Thomas Coke
'God's Good News to the World'

JOHN AARON

© Day One Publications 2021

ISBN 978-1-84625-705-6

British Library Cataloguing in Publication Data available

Published by Day One Publications
Ryelands Road, Leominster, HR6 8NZ
Telephone 01568 613 740
North America Toll Free 888 329 6630
email—sales@dayone.co.uk
web site—www.dayone.co.uk

The portrait on page 1 is from the collections of the Oxford Centre for Methodism
and Church History, Oxford Brookes University, Oxford, U.K. Used with permission.

Cover design by smallprint

Printed by Cambrian Printers Ltd

Contents

List of Illustrations

Series Preface

Mission and Vision: Welsh greats who changed the world for Christ is a series of very readable short biographies of men and women from Wales who have had an amazing influence for good.

Whatever your age or wherever you come from, it is hoped that these real-life stories will inspire you to delve more deeply into their lives. They are meant to excite younger people as well as older readers to take an interest in history and especially in individuals who are so little remembered or even neglected but who have made a significant impact not only in Wales but more generally throughout Britain and beyond.

It is our earnest prayer that the Lord would use these biographical sketches to stimulate, encourage and challenge those who read them to live to the glory of God and the advancement of his kingdom.

Philip H Eveson
Chairman of the Bryntirion Press Committee

Preface

I n his 1985 biography of Thomas Coke, Cyril Davey wrote:

> *Next to John Wesley himself, who called the Methodists into being, the most significant and formative figure in Methodism's first hundred years is unquestionably Dr Thomas Coke.*

There is plenty of evidence to support such a statement, as a glance at the Timeline on the next page will confirm. Over a hundred years before Davey's book appeared, another historian of Methodism, Thomas Jackson, wrote of Coke in the same vein:

> *His services in connexion with the Methodist Missions were marked by an energy, disinterestedness, and perseverance which can never be forgotten; and in importance and success they were second only to those of the venerated man whom he owned as his father in the Lord.*

But Jackson was wrong in his prediction: despite all his achievements, two hundred years after his death, Thomas Coke is largely forgotten even in Wales, the land of his birth. It is hoped that this short biography will help to correct this.

Thomas Coke Timeline

1747	Born in Brecon, Wales
1764	Attends Jesus College, Oxford
1768	Graduates B.A.
1770	Mayor of Brecon. Obtains M.A. from Oxford
1771	Curate in South Petherton, Somerset
1775	Obtains doctorate in Civil Law
1776	Meets John Wesley
1777	Driven out of his parish because of his 'Methodist ways'
1782	Elected President of the Irish Methodist Conference
1784	Draws up the *Deed of Declaration* defining the Methodist Conference
1784	'Set apart' by John Wesley as Superintendent of American Methodist work. Sails for America
1784	Elected Superintendent, jointly with Francis Asbury, over the American Methodists. Later styled 'Bishop'
1786	Writes *'Address to the Pious and Benevolent'*, proposing an annual subscription for the support of overseas missions
1786	Second visit to America, and the first of his four visits to the West Indies
1791	Death of John Wesley
1791-1813	Holds the position of Secretary of the British Methodist Conference whenever he is not abroad, and is elected its president for 1797 and 1805
1795	Draws up the *Plan of Pacification* and oversees the separation of Methodists from the Church of England
1799	Initiates missions to Irish speakers in Ireland and Welsh speakers in Wales
1804	Returns from America for the last time after nine visits

1805	Marries Penelope Goulding Smith from Bradford-on-Avon. She dies in 1811
1811	Marries Anne Loxdale of Liverpool. She dies in 1812
1814	Embarks on a new mission to South East Asia. Dies on the voyage, 3 May, and is buried at sea, north of Madagascar

Chapter 1: A Brecon Boy

Brecon lies among the Brecon Beacons at the point where the Honddu river joins the Usk, giving the town its Welsh name: Aberhonddu which means 'the mouth of the river Honddu'. Overlooking the town is the long ridge of Pen-y-fan, the highest point of the Beacons. Brecon was the richest and largest town in Wales in the eighteenth century. Its location and history meant that it was mainly an English-speaking town, surrounded by Welsh-speaking rural areas. It lay on the direct coach route from London to Carmarthen and was the commercial centre for most of mid-Wales. Its many coaching inns catered for all the travellers passing through and for the hundreds of customers crowding the streets, twice a week, on busy market days. Many fine buildings lined the High Street, the homes of wealthy financiers and lawyers and the properties also of the gentry of the surrounding countryside, who maintained their townhouses. At this time, Brecon was known as 'the Bath of Wales'. Its population was less than three thousand but its growing prosperity had made it the cultural and fashionable centre for the whole of South Wales. Its 'season' included many balls, concerts and theatrical performances, held in the playhouses of the town.

Governing the affairs of this successful borough were the town councillors, known as 'burgesses'. One of these was Bartholomew Coke (pronounced 'Cook'). He was a man of considerable property and wealth, owning the popular inn, 'The Leg of Mutton', a few doors up from his house in the High Street. But he was also an apothecary by profession, one who would prescribe as well as dispense the medicines for his customers. Indeed, it was said of him that if patients were in his care they had no need of a doctor. He was trusted by the gentry of the county as their doctor and he also, just as conscientiously, cared for the poor of the town. The Gwynne family of Garth were his clients, as was Howell Harris of Trefeca. Benjamin Coke was twice elected mayor of the town, or rather 'the Bailiff', according to the title used in Brecon; he was also a faithful member of the Church of England, as religious in the home as in the church. There is no evidence that the family could speak Welsh.

St Mary's Church, Brecon

Childhood and Education

Thomas was born to Bartholomew and Ann Coke on 28 September 1747. He was their only child. Two other boys had been born to them before Thomas, but neither survived infancy. He grew up, a much-loved child, in 'the quiet and unemotional atmosphere of family devotions, prayer-book religion and parish worship.' St Mary's, the parish church, was only a few minutes' walk down the High Street and would have been as familiar to him as his own home.

Along High Street, in the opposite direction to the church, down the hill, and then across the bridge, would have brought you, just as it does today, to Christ College, a grammar school established by Henry VIII in 1541. Here Thomas was educated, learning sufficient Greek and Latin to gain entrance to Jesus College, Oxford University in 1764. His parents intended that he should follow a career in the Church of England and had great hopes that, with his background of wealth, culture and learning, he would rise to some prominence. Such hopes were not misplaced in that, at sixteen years of age, Thomas was intelligent, mature, cheerful and well-mannered. Though a short man, just over five foot, he was good-looking. 'Short, sturdy, round-faced, ruddy-cheeked, he had dark curly hair and a flashing smile. He was open by temperament, a good companion with a swift wit and easy conversation.'

At university he had to fight against the current philosophy of the day, that of Deism, which believed in an impersonal God, remote and detached from his creation. The truths of Christianity which he had accepted from his parents – the doctrines of the Trinity, the sinfulness of mankind, the Incarnation of the Son of God, his atoning death as Saviour of the world, the existence of Heaven and Hell – all these were questioned, even ridiculed by most of those around him. Their scepticism had a strong effect on him. It was only by much study, by maintaining the morning prayers and the chapel attendance of his upbringing, and by reading Christian books, that he was confirmed in the orthodox truths of the faith. In his own words, 'I had the struggle to myself; I knew no one who believed.' He could consider his future as a priest in the knowledge that he was no hypocrite; the doctrines, teachings and form of worship of the Established Church, which it would be his duty to teach others, were those which he himself believed with all his heart.

But he was not yet converted. His religion was sincere, moral and orthodox, but he knew nothing of an awakening of his heart by the Holy Spirit; he had no experience of the forgiveness of his sins; he enjoyed no fellowship with the living Christ.

Having gained his B.A. in 1768, he returned to live at home while waiting to obtain the degree of M.A. At Brecon his abilities were already well-known and acknowledged. He was appointed a 'burgess', joining his father in the ranks of the town's Common Council. A year later, in 1770, and again following in his father's footsteps, he was elected to the office of Bailiff of Brecon, at the age of twenty-three. In the same year he obtained his M.A. from Oxford and was ordained a deacon of the Church of England.

But suddenly, and for no apparent reason, his rapid ascent to the higher ranks of the Church came to a halt. The Member of Parliament for Brecon had obtained his seat through the support of the Coke family and it was thought that he could find a suitable appointment for the young man, but nothing was forthcoming. Even more hopeful was the patronage of Lord North, another family friend, who was soon to be the Prime Minister, but he also did nothing. Coke was forced to curb his ambition and wait patiently.

Chapter 2: A Curate Converted

A Somerset Curate

Coke was eventually appointed in 1771 as an assistant curate at South Petherton, a small town in Somerset, about eight miles west of Yeovil. His responsibilities as curate were light at first which meant that he could return often to Brecon to carry out his mayoral duties. The fact that he was mayor of such an important town added considerably to his

South Petherton

social status in his new situation. Together with his cheerful and winsome personality, this soon gained him an entry into the social life of the town, as did his skill (gained from his university years) in dancing and playing whist. In 1772, he was ordained a priest of the Church of England by the Bishop of St David's at the Bishop's Palace in Abergwili and on the death of his father in the following year he became a very wealthy young man.

As a priest Coke could now serve at the Communion Table, and his clerical duties increased greatly, particularly in that his vicar, Robert Twyford, suffered from ill-health. He began to appreciate the seriousness of his responsibility for the spiritual well-being of the souls under his care, and he gave more and more attention to his sermons. His zealous preaching soon filled the church. More room was needed for the congregation and as his parishioners could not be persuaded to build a new gallery he did so at his own expense. He still had high hopes for preferment in the Church and this led him to follow a course of legal studies, which eventually resulted in his gaining the degree of D.C.L. (Doctor of Civil Law) from Oxford in 1775. From that time on he was generally known as Dr Thomas Coke.

Sometime in the period between 1773 and 1776, Thomas Coke was born again. When exactly is not known, but it was certainly not a sudden conversion. Coke's study of the Bible as he prepared his sermons convinced him that true religion consisted in a change of heart and not merely in any outward performance of ritual and ceremony. He then came across *An Alarm to the Unconverted*, a book by the Puritan, Joseph Alleine, which confirmed him in these new thoughts. He then met and began to associate with James Browne, the vicar of Kingston St Mary, near Taunton. This godly man lent him some books by the Rev. John Fletcher of Madeley, Shropshire. These particularly helped Coke; they seemed to him to be written for someone in his condition exactly. It was a great surprise for him to hear that this Fletcher was one of the despised and fanatical Methodists and a friend of the worst of them – a man who broke all the rules of church order, who travelled around the country preaching in the open air and gathering crowds of deluded enthusiasts about him – the Rev. John Wesley. A still greater surprise was to hear that godly old James Browne was also a friend of this arch-Methodist and that Wesley often visited him when preaching in the area.

Ironically, a little before this time, before Coke came to realize that he had ever met a Methodist, his parish at South Petherton had begun to suspect that he was one himself. The dancing and whist-playing had been long forgotten as he began to give a series of evening lectures in the week and to hold meetings in people's homes. Most of all, his preaching changed. His sermons were no longer on morality, standards and behaviour, but on the sin of the heart, the need of forgiveness and, pre-eminently, the grace of God in Jesus Christ; they were not now read from manuscripts but preached without notes, and with a warmth of heart and zeal that was completely new to the people of South Petherton. More worrying still, other people, from parishes further afield, began to arrive at their church on a Sunday, drawn by what they heard of the preaching of the young curate. In a letter to John Fletcher at this time, Coke wrote:

> *I do humbly beg that you will pray for me. I am sure you will grant me that favour when I inform you that (as nearly as I can guess) a thousand or more immortal souls come to me on every Lord's day in the afternoon to receive their portion of the bread of everlasting life.*

At some point during this period, as he was walking through a field, on the way to another cottage service, he prayed earnestly for an assurance for himself of that salvation he was about to preach to others. Later, mid-sermon, he suddenly received all that he had prayed for. He was filled with 'an instantaneous assurance of the pardon of sins' together with a sense of profound peace and of great purposes to be fulfilled in the future.

The increasing numbers in his services overflowed into the church porch and out into the churchyard. There was not enough bread and wine to go round on a Communion Sunday, usually held three or four times a year. He therefore decided that communion would be celebrated every Sunday, a decision that shocked his traditional parishioners. The opposition in the parish became more and more open.

First Meeting with John Wesley

John Wesley was due to preach at Taunton on Tuesday 13 August 1776 and then to stay the night with James Browne. Browne invited Coke to come over to meet him. The two men conversed all evening and then again through the morning. Wesley describes the meeting in his *Journal* for this date:

> *I preached at Taunton, and afterwards went with Mr Brown to Kingston. The large old parsonage-house is pleasantly situated close to the church-yard, just fit for a contemplative man. Here I found a Clergyman, Dr. Coke, late Gentleman Commoner of Jesus College in Oxford, who came twenty miles on purpose. I had much conversation with him; and an union then began, which I trust shall never end.*

John Wesley

The twenty-eight year old Coke was just as much taken by the seventy-three year old Methodist. He wrote that he found him 'mild and easy of access, with an appearance of happiness'. After describing his troubles in his parish, he was advised 'to go on in the same path, doing all the good he could, visiting from house to house, omitting no part of his clerical duty; and to avoid every reasonable ground of offence.'

Dismissed from South Petherton

During the next year Coke tried to follow this advice but his spiritual experiences had resulted in such zeal, combined at times with impetuous and hasty judgments, that the parish divisions were only deepening. He announced in the Sunday services the places he would visit during the week in order to preach – in homes, barns and out of doors. His preaching tours would often take him into adjoining parishes. He also began the practice of singing hymns in the services, even the hymns of Charles Wesley!

Although complaints against him had been sent to his vicar, Twyford, perhaps because of his ill-health, had not stepped in to restrain him. But when Twyford died in 1776, his successor, Thomas Goddard, ordered Coke that all 'disorderly practices' should be brought to an end immediately. Coke took no notice of the instruction. As a result, in the middle of the morning service on Easter Sunday, when Coke was about to begin his sermon, Goddard stood up and announced to the church that the Rev. Dr Thomas Coke was dismissed as curate. The dismissal had clearly been carefully planned. When Coke stepped down from the pulpit a new curate, already appointed, stood up in his place and began to preach. As Coke left the church, the church bells were rung, celebrating the town's victory over their unwanted curate.

> *These insults roused his Welsh blood; and he determined, with more spirit than prudence, to take his stand near the church on the two following Sundays, and to preach to the people when they came out, for the purpose of vindicating himself, gratifying his adherents, and exhorting his opponents to repentance. These … were so provoked at this, that they collected stones, for the purpose of pelting him, on his second exhibition; and the Doctor would hardly have escaped without some serious injury, if a young lady and her brother, whom the people knew and respected, had not placed themselves one on each side of him.*

Joining the Methodists

Coke was now certain that his future lay with John Wesley's Methodists. He looked forward to using all his influence and abilities in furthering their cause. At this time the English Methodists numbered about 38,000 people, served by about 150 travelling preachers. These preachers were under the personal direction of Wesley. Together they made up the Methodist 'Connexion' which had been in existence for nearly forty years. Wesley was determined that the

Connexion should always remain within the Established Church. He therefore called the gatherings of his people in their localities 'societies' and not churches; they were not to hold meetings at the same time as the parish church services; the preachers were not to administer the sacraments among the societies – only clergymen associated with the Methodists were allowed to do so.

In his Journal for 19 October 1777, Wesley wrote:

> *I went forward to Taunton, with Dr. Coke, who, being dismissed from his Curacy, has bid adieu to his honourable name, and determined to cast in his lot with us.*

Coke spent some weeks in Bristol, meeting with the sailors, miners and traders of the Bristol society, and beginning to appreciate, as he listened to their spiritual conversations, how young he was in the faith and how much he had to learn. But John Wesley had very definite plans for this able, talented clergyman who had so suddenly emerged among them.

Thomas Coke (aged 33)

Chapter 3: Wesley's Right-hand Man

A Leader among the Methodists

John Wesley, at seventy-four years of age, was having to consider how his Connexion was to develop in the future. He was determined to maintain his itinerant way of life but realized he could no longer visit all his societies throughout the British Isles regularly. He needed someone to represent him in this work. He also required help with all the legal and administrative side of the movement and there was the need for a deputy to be permanently in charge at 'The Foundery', City Road, the London headquarters of the Connexion. Wesley was also considering whether or not he should appoint his own successor. Up to this time, these responsibilities had been divided between his brother Charles, his greatest help and supporter from the very beginning of the work, and John Fletcher of Madeley, the most accomplished writer of the movement. Charles, however, was only four years younger than John and, happy in his family life, was content to remain mostly in London. Fletcher had already turned down an offer to be Wesley's successor; his health was deteriorating; he was glad to be out of the public eye and wished to commit more of his time to writing.

From the very first meeting with Coke, Wesley realized his capabilities. No one else in the movement had such a rank in society or such wealth behind him; no other clergyman was so free from family, church or other commitments; no one had more zeal and energy for the task. Instead of stationing him, like the other preachers, in a Methodist 'circuit' (a geographical region), with responsibility for all the societies in the region, Wesley took him as a travelling companion so that he could learn how to superintend the various societies. Wesley would send him where there was any particular need. Coke visited the societies in Ireland regularly, eventually alternating with Wesley so that an annual visitation was kept up. His links with Ireland were to develop so successfully that he was appointed leader of the well-established Methodist work there, and he held the office of President of the Irish Conference, visiting them every year for thirty-two years, from 1782 until his death.

Wesley's Chapel, City Road, London, completed in 1778
The house on the right was John Wesley's home when he was in London

In 1778 Coke was appointed to London. The London Methodists were building a chapel to replace the old Foundery. It was called the New Chapel, City Road, and Charles Wesley was in charge. Charles was more of a High Churchman than John and on a Sunday would only allow clergymen to preach in the London Methodist chapels. At the New Chapel, therefore, the only Sunday preachers were Charles himself, Coke, and another clergyman, John Richardson. When we remember that many of Wesley's itinerant helpers were better preachers than these three men, and that most of them had laboured in the Connexion for many more years than Coke, it is not surprising that a degree of jealousy and suspicion of him should now arise in some minds. His influence with Wesley, his sudden rise to leadership in Ireland, London, and the country generally, together with his considerable self-confidence and, at times, his rather officious manner, all these combined to suggest to many that he was a deeply ambitious man. This is a point that will have to be considered later. It is sufficient now merely to note that those who recognized his commitment, his ready use of his own money for all his expenses in the work, his willingness to follow Wesley's directions humbly and obediently, were more than ready to accept Wesley's high view of him.

As the only one of the Methodist clergy who was legally trained, Coke had to deal with many of the legal problems that arose within the Connexion. Whenever any conflict arose between lay preachers and clergy, or when disagreements over the terms of the trust deeds of chapels, or over the right to appoint preachers for the chapels, became heated, Wesley would send Coke as a 'trouble-shooter'. Some of these conflicts involved considerable discussions with lawyers and others. He would occasionally publish pamphlets to inform the societies of the issues involved. Alongside these administrative duties his preaching tours continued. One historian, in painting a picture of Coke on one of his journeys in 1783, provides a typical example of how so many of the Methodist societies came into being:

> Dr Coke was passing through Stafford, and, while dining at the inn, sent the bellman round to announce to the inhabitants that he would preach in the market place. Jeremiah Brettell, his companion, took a table from the hostelry; the doctor mounted; the people came; all listened with deep attention; and some expressed a wish for the visit to be repeated. Soon after, a little society was formed, which in 1784 consisted of sixteen members.

By 1784 John Wesley realized that no one individual could replace him at the head of the Society and that he had to set the future of the Connexion on a firmer footing. He had, since 1744, been meeting yearly with some of the clergymen and lay preachers to discuss the affairs of the Methodists. The numbers of the select few who were invited to attend this 'Conference' grew until eventually all preachers who wished to attend were free to do so, and the Conference became the general assembly of the movement. The Methodist chapels, of which there were 359 in existence by 1784, were required legally, after the death of the two Wesleys, to be held in trust:

> for the sole use of such persons as might be appointed at the yearly conference of the people called Methodists, provided that the said persons preached no other doctrines than those contained in Wesley's Notes on the New Testament, and in his four volumes of sermons.

But, as yet, there was no legal definition of the term 'conference of the people called Methodists'. Wesley asked Coke to draw up such a definition and to provide a suitable constitution for the Conference. Coke conferred with able lawyers and having drawn up a draft of a deed, presented it to Wesley. In Coke's opinion, every preacher in full connection with the

John Wesley preaching in the City Road Chapel, London
Thomas Coke is directly behind him, fourth from the left in the third row down

Methodists should be a member of the Conference. Wesley disagreed and, without advice from Coke, made his own selection of a hundred out of the one hundred and ninety-two preachers appointed at the time to the sixty-nine circuits throughout the British Isles. All the preachers might still attend, confer and discuss, but the final ratification of all decisions would be made by the one hundred named representatives. This *Deed of Declaration*, as might have been expected, was the cause of much disappointment and grumbling amongst those passed over. Many of those omitted in the list came to the conclusion, wrongly and unfairly, that Coke was the author of their exclusion. At the Conference of 1784, however, Wesley explained his reasons for setting the number and for his choice of men, and the Deed was accepted. It was now laid out in law that after Wesley's death, Conference would become the legal government of the Methodist Connexion. Many remained resentful of the changes made and, in the event, nearly thirty preachers withdrew from the Connexion.

Chapter 4: A Bishop in America

Wesley had sent two preachers to America in 1769. In 1771, two more men, Richard Wright and Francis Asbury were sent. The latter worked among the villages and scattered plantations rather than in large towns. By 1773 the first Wesleyan Conference in America was held, where it appeared that there were about a thousand members in the different societies. The War of Independence interrupted all progress, particularly so because Wesley published a pamphlet against the rebellion, arguing for Britain's right to impose taxes on America. The Methodists in America became deeply unpopular. All the missionary preachers had to flee the country, with the exception of Francis Asbury who went into hiding for two years. By the time of America's victory in the War of Independence, the Methodists of the country were ministered to by American preachers alone, and with such success that by 1784 they numbered over eighty preachers and about 15,000 members. But in one respect, their situation had become desperate. The vast majority of English clergymen had returned to Britain. Of the American Methodists who had been appointed to preach, not one had been ordained. The result was that it was hardly possible for a Methodist to receive communion from any authorized person anywhere in the newly-formed United States.

The First Methodist Ordinations

John Wesley's response was decisive. In Bristol, on 1 September 1784, he met with two of his preachers who had already been set apart to work in America, Richard Whatcoat and Thomas Vasey, and, with Thomas Coke assisting, he ordained them. As Church of England ministers they were now eligible to administer the sacraments. Wesley's entry in his *Journal* shows his determination:

Wednesday, 1 September. Being now clear in my own mind, I took a step which I had long weighed in my mind, and appointed Mr. Whatcoat and Mr. Vasey to go and serve the desolate sheep in America.

On the following day, he appointed Coke as Superintendent over all Methodist work in America. The express purpose of this office was that Coke might now ordain further ministers once he arrived in the States.

These actions were understood by Wesley to be the very necessary and pragmatic steps that had to be taken to cater for his people's needs in America, but they were the occasion of a controversy that has still not been resolved by Methodist historians. In the Church of England the office of bishop outranks the office of presbyter (or 'priest' which is the term used in the Book of Common Prayer). In particular, it is only a bishop who has the authority to ordain laymen, appointing them first as deacons and then as presbyters/priests. For some time, however, Wesley had taken the view that there was no distinction in the Bible between the terms 'bishop' and 'presbyter/priest' or 'elder'. The two Greek names, he believed, describe different aspects of the same office. The Greek word for bishop (*episkopos*) emphasizes the work of overseeing or superintending, and the Greek word for presbyter/priest (*presbyteros* which is usually translated 'elder' in the New Testament) denotes the respect due to the office. As a Church of England presbyter/priest, Wesley therefore believed that he had the same right as a Church of England bishop to ordain new ministers. This, however, was the first occasion for him to do this and, whatever his own convictions might have been, it was an act that contravened the Established Church order that bishops alone had the right to ordain. And in his subsequent step of appointing Coke to an office that carried the right to ordain others, though he might insist that Coke should be given the name 'superintendent', he was in reality appointing him to the position of a Church of England bishop! Involved in the action also was the incongruous situation of Wesley, a presbyter/priest, appointing Coke, also a presbyter/priest, to this higher position of superintendent/bishop.

Coke had agreed fully with Wesley in these actions. He had earlier written to him:

> The more maturely I consider the subject, the more expedient it appears to me, that the power of ordaining others should be received by me from you, by the imposition of your hands; and that you should lay hands on brother Whatcoat and brother Vasey, for the following reasons;
>
> (i) It seems to me the most scriptural way, and most agreeable to the practice of the primitive churches.
>
> (ii) I may want all the influence, in America, which you can throw into my scale.
>
> …I am satisfied that an authority, formally received from you, will be fully admitted; and that my exercising the office of ordination, without that formal authority, may be disputed, and perhaps, on other accounts, opposed. I think you have tried me too often to doubt, whether I will, in any degree, use the power you are pleased to invest me with, farther than I believe absolutely necessary for the prosperity of the work.

When these steps became known, there was an immediate reaction. Charles Wesley was convinced of the implications involved, and deplored it bitterly. He wrote to a friend:

> I can scarcely yet believe it that, in his eighty-second year, my brother, my old, intimate friend and companion, should have assumed the Episcopal character, ordained elders, consecrated a bishop, and sent him to ordain our lay preachers in America! I was then in Bristol, at his elbow; yet he never gave me the least hint of his intention. How was he surprised into so rash an action? He certainly persuaded himself that it was right. Lord Mansfield told me last year that ordination was separation. This, my brother does not, and will not see; or that he has renounced the principles and practice of his whole life.

It is this question as to whether or not John Wesley wished the Methodists to separate from the Established Church that has perplexed historians ever since. There were to be five other occasions when he ordained some of his lay preachers, men set aside to labour in Scotland, on the mission field, or in parts of England where there were no sympathetic clergymen, yet his respect and loyalty to the Church of England were such that he would never consider himself as a Dissenter or Nonconformist. A future leader of nineteenth century Methodism, Jabez Bunting, wrote of him: 'He looked one way, while every stroke of his oar took him another.' Others have written of Wesley's inconsistency, of 'the actions of an old man', or of 'evidence that his reasoning faculty had greatly failed.' But many, anxious to defend Wesley, have argued that he was persuaded against his will by Coke, and that he gave in to Coke's demands, because of his love and respect for him. The familiar prejudice against Coke has often been raised again at this point. Thus:

> With the highest respect for Dr Coke, and his general excellencies, it is no detraction to assert, that he was dangerously ambitious, and that the height of his ambition was a desire to be a bishop.

As mentioned previously, this claim that Coke was a man driven by ambition will be addressed later.

Coke's First Visit to America

Unaware of the arguments that he left behind him, Coke sailed from Bristol on 18 September 1784 and arrived six and a half weeks later in New York. After two days and two sermons in New York, he set off for Delaware where he was to meet Asbury. He was unsure what kind of reception he would receive, coming as the representative of the Established Church in Britain to command and direct the gathered Methodist churches of a land that had just lately thrown off the yoke of their British rulers. In a small settlement called Barrett's Chapel, in the forests of Delaware, he preached to 'a noble congregation' that had gathered to hear him. After the sermon a sturdy, robust man, with clothes worn by long miles of travelling, rose to greet him. It was Asbury, and he addressed the congregation: 'If we cannot have Mr Wesley himself we rejoice to have his right-hand man.' Coke's response was similar, 'I exceedingly revere Mr Asbury, he has so much wisdom and consideration, so much meekness and love and, under all this, though hardly to be perceived, so much command and authority.' The two men became firm friends, and although that friendship was severely tested and strained over the next thirty years it was never broken.

FRANCIS ASBURY.

THOMAS COKE.

The two men agreed to call a Conference of the American Methodists for 24 December at Baltimore, Maryland. In the meantime Asbury drew up a circuit of about a thousand miles for Coke to ride on horseback, preaching at various Methodist preaching stations on the way. This was in fact the reverse trip of what Asbury himself had taken in order to meet Coke in Delaware. This experience was unlike anything that Coke had undertaken up to that time. He found himself preaching in the midst of ancient forests, 'with scores, and sometimes hundreds of horses tied to the trees.' He wrote in his *Journal*:

Sometimes a most noble vista, of half a mile or a mile in length, would open between the lofty pines: sometimes the tender fawns and hinds would suddenly appear, and on seeing or hearing us, would glance through the woods, or vanish away … The deep green of the pines, the bright transparent green of the oaks, and the fine white of the dogwood trees, with other trees and shrubs, form such a complication of beauties as is indescribable to those who have only lived in countries that are almost entirely cultivated.

He could not fail to be struck also by the success that had attended the preaching of the frontier Methodist 'circuit-riders': 'I am daily filled with surprise in meeting with such large congregations as I am favoured with, in the midst of vast wilderness, and wonder from whence they come!' He noted in a later entry in his Journal that on this, his first tour of America, he had baptized more children and adults than he would have done in his whole life if he had stayed in an English parish.

Bishop Thomas Coke

At Baltimore, sixty preachers had gathered. They realized that their purpose was to determine the nature and future of the Methodist Church in America. They firstly accepted the form of church government and the manner of worship for the Methodists in America, which Wesley had directed. On Christmas Day, 1784, Coke ordained Asbury as a deacon, and on the following day he ordained him as a presbyter. Then, on 27 December, he ordained him as a co-superintendent with himself over the American Methodists. But Asbury had wisely decided that he would not be a superintendent only on Wesley's nomination and insisted on a unanimous election by the Conference before either Coke or he exercised this office. Asbury summarized the main decisions taken:

It was agreed to form ourselves into an Episcopal Church, and to have superintendents, elders and deacons. When the conference was seated, Dr Coke and myself were unanimously elected to the superintendency of the Church, and my ordination followed.

They constituted themselves as the Methodist Episcopal Church of America. By this action they became the first Methodists formally to separate from the Established Church, and therefore, of course, to separate also from their parent Methodist body in Britain.

Thomas Coke ordaining Francis Asbury

At their first meeting the two men had agreed to work together to establish a school, or college, on the plan of the Methodist school at Kingswood, Bristol. Before they met at the Conference, they had already collected more than a thousand pounds of subscriptions for it. Coke bought four acres of ground at a site about twenty-eight miles from Baltimore. The college was named Cokesbury College, after its two founders.

No Episcopal church had ever been governed by 'superintendents'. It was inevitable that sooner or later Coke and Asbury would be termed 'bishops'. This was certainly the case by September 1788, when Wesley, who was getting worried by the increasingly independent stance the American church was taking, wrote to Asbury:

> *Both the Doctor and you differ from me. I study to be little: you study to be great. I creep, you strut along. I found a school: you a College! Nay, and call it after your own names! O beware, do not seek to be something!*
>
> *…How can you, how dare you, suffer yourself to be called Bishop? I shudder, I start at the very thought. Men may call me a knave, or a fool, a rascal, a scoundrel, and I am content, but they shall never by my consent call me a bishop! For my sake, for God's sake, for Christ's sake put a full end to this!*

In the second paragraph, Wesley again betrays his inconsistency. He had clearly wished Coke and Asbury to act as bishops, that is, to proceed to ordain some of the lay preachers. What he could not accept, knowing, perhaps, the

Cokesbury College, Abingdon, Baltimore, Maryland

opposition that it would bring down upon him from the Established Church at home, was that they did this under the name of 'bishop', rather than the more innocuous name of 'superintendent' which he had chosen.

Slavery

Wherever he travelled on his circuits, Coke encountered black slaves. America's population at the time was three million; one million of these were slaves. Coke was appalled by their situation and suffering and, with his usual ardour and vehemence, preached against slavery often and prepared a petition to Congress for the emancipation of slaves. This was, in fact, four years before William Wilberforce began his own campaign against the slave trade with a speech in the House of Commons in 1789.

On 25 May 1785 Coke and Asbury visited and dined with George Washington, who had recently resigned from his position as commander-in-chief of the American army. They presented him with a copy of the petition and asked if he would sign it. Washington explained that it would be inappropriate for him to sign, because of his position, but he assured them that he agreed with it. Asbury and Coke required the Methodists to set their slaves free, and several of them did so, but Coke, with perhaps more zeal than wisdom, pressed the matter so vehemently, that he provoked violent opposition. One of his sermons on the topic so incensed some of his hearers that they decided to ambush him. One woman, a slave owner, promised them fifty pounds if they would give 'that little Doctor' a hundred lashes, but he escaped their wrath. At the beginning of his second visit to America in 1787, Asbury warned him that the opposition to his views was so great that it was impeding the progress of Methodism. Coke realized that he had acted indiscreetly and consented to let the question of emancipation rest.

Wesley and Coke had intended that this first visit to America was to be one of a few weeks only. After the Baltimore Conference, however, Coke continued for many months riding the circuits in New Jersey, Pennsylvania, Virginia and North Carolina. In the event, he was away from Britain for ten months (September 1784 to July 1785). The cost of the passage to America, for himself and for Whatcoat and Vasey, he had paid for himself, as he did all his expenses while travelling around the country. This was to be his practice throughout his years of journeying. The wealth acquired by the property-owning apothecary of Brecon was being used by his son for the world-wide extension of the Christian gospel.

Return to Britain

Coke arrived back in Britain just in time to attend the July 1785 Methodist Conference. He returned when the arguments over Wesley's act of ordination were at their fiercest. Many put the blame at his door, Charles Wesley in particular. The latter had been incensed by a sermon, preached by Coke in America but published on both sides of the Atlantic. Inspired by the sense of unity he had perceived in the new American republic, by the failure, as he saw it, of the Church of England there, and by the heartening progress of the American Methodist Church, Coke had expressed a hope that the Methodists in Britain might soon follow the lead of their American brethren in separating from the Established Church. As sometimes happened, he had allowed his enthusiasm to run away with him and had been unguarded in his expressions. These tensions between Coke and the Wesley brothers over the nature of the Methodist Connexion remained right up to the deaths of Charles and John in 1788 and 1791 respectively. Nor were they finally resolved within the Connexion itself, of course, until the Methodist Church formally separated from the Established Church in 1795.

GOING TO CONFERENCE.

An American Methodist circuit-rider

Chapter 5: Committed to Missions

The First Call for Wesleyan Missions

On Coke's second meeting with Wesley, after his expulsion from South Petherton, the latter had told him, 'Brother, go out, go out, and preach the gospel to all the world'. From the very beginning of his association with the Methodists, therefore, Coke was convinced of the responsibility of all Christians to take the good news to all the world. Even when he was occupied with drawing up the *Deed of Declaration* for Wesley, he pondered over what should be done. Late in 1783, jointly with a local preacher from York, Thomas Parker, he published '*A Plan of the Society for the Establishing of Missions among the Heathen*'. The *Plan* suggested the establishing of a body that would finance and send out missionaries to the heathen nations:

> *The spirit of a missionary must be of the most zealous, most devoted, and self-denying kind; nor is anything more required to constitute a missionary for the heathen nations, than good sense, integrity, great piety, and amazing zeal. Men, possessing all these qualifications in a high degree, we have among us; and we doubt not but some of these will accept of the arduous undertaking, not counting their lives dear, if they may but promote the kingdom of Christ, and the present and eternal welfare of their fellow creatures.*

Initial subscriptions of up to ninety pounds had already been collected, and it is significant that among the first twenty-five subscribers to the Society was John Fletcher of Madeley. However, it does not seem that anything came from this first attempt, perhaps because the *Plan* failed to gain Wesley's support. What is worth noting is that this suggestion came eight years before the publication which is usually considered as the initial spur for the foundation of eighteenth century missionary societies, namely *An Enquiry into the Obligations of Christians to use means for the Conversion of the Heathen* by the Baptist pastor and cobbler, William Carey.

A little over two years later, after his experiences in America and motivated, in particular, by his knowledge of the condition of the African slaves and of their response to the preaching of the gospel, Coke tried again. The title of this second pamphlet was *An Address to the Pious and Benevolent, proposing an annual subscription for the support of Missionaries*. He had learnt his lesson, in that he prefaced the work with a commendation by Wesley:

> *I greatly approve of your proposal for raising a subscription in order to send missionaries to the Highlands of Scotland, the islands of Jersey and Guernsey, the Leeward Islands, Quebec, Nova Scotia, and Newfoundland. It is not easy to conceive the extreme want there is, in all these places, of men that will not count their lives dear to themselves, so that they testify the gospel of the grace of God.*

The countries mentioned were those where a few Methodist lay preachers were already active and experiencing varying degrees of success. In the Conference of 1786 Coke made an impassioned plea to the gathered preachers for their support, at least to the extent of sending a preacher to the West Indies:

> *Our country is enriched by the labours of the poor slaves who till the soil, and the least compensation we can make is to enrich them with the riches of grace. But the grand consideration is the value of their souls … utterly despised by all the world except the Missionaries and the Moravians.*

The decision to send William Warrener to work in Antigua was made all the easier for Conference by the fact that Coke undertook to pay for his passage. Two other men, John Clarke and William Hammet, were to accompany Warrener and Coke on what was to be Coke's second visit to America. These two had been appointed to work in Newfoundland, and that was to be the first point of call on the voyage.

This decision by the 1786 Conference to accept Coke's plan of subscription is considered to be the step that defines the beginning of Methodist Missionary work. It is true that men had been sent by Conference to Nova Scotia and Newfoundland some years before, but this was regarded as an extension of the work in America rather than as a separate mission field. It was given to Thomas Coke to introduce the first plan of missionary work, to finance the sending out of its first missionaries, to accompany them to their stations and, as we shall see, to direct the work in an ever increasing number of countries. In fact, for the next thirty years, all Methodist planning, directing and financing of missionary work was undertaken, almost single-handedly, by Thomas Coke himself. Not until 1818, four years after his death, was the Wesleyan Methodist Missionary Society formally established.

The First Methodist Work in the West Indies

Nathaniel Gilbert, the son of a wealthy planter, was the Speaker of the House of Assembly in Antigua, West Indies. He visited England in 1756 and sought an interview with Wesley. He was converted and joined the Methodist society. On returning to Antigua in 1758 he maintained a service on Sundays in his own house, praying with, and preaching to, any who wished to join him. Encouraged by his success, he began to preach to the black slaves. Many despised him for this and he soon lost his congregation of white colonials, but it resulted in the formation of a Methodist society. At the time of his death in 1774 this was made up of some two hundred slaves.

In 1778 a shipwright called John Baxter, who worked in the royal docks at Chatham and was a leader among the Methodists, moved to Antigua to work for the government there. He took over the leadership of the society. He wrote to Wesley, 'The old standers desire me to inform you that you have many children in Antigua, whom you never saw.' By 1786 there were two thousand members in the society and Baxter, with the help of the slaves, built a chapel that could hold a congregation of nearly two thousand.

He wrote to Wesley, pleading for a preacher to be sent to the island. At this time, all of Wesley's resources were engaged in maintaining the societies at home and in America. As we saw in the case of Coke's *Plan*, the concept of global mission had not yet gained an acceptance. But Coke, during his first visit to America and hearing of Baxter's needs, had written to him, suggesting that he journey from Antigua to meet him in Baltimore. Baxter did so and Coke promptly ordained him, so that on his return to the island Baxter could continue his work with the status of an ordained clergyman. This ordination Coke undertook on his own initiative, not having corresponded with Wesley. Coke and Baxter were to meet again much sooner than they could ever have imagined.

A Fateful Voyage

Coke and the three new appointees set sail on 24 September 1786. Coke's first crossing of the Atlantic had taken six weeks but this voyage was to last almost three months. The ship nearly beached when rounding the Kent coast, it narrowly escaped a collision with a brig near Land's End, and once they reached open sea they were beset by continual storms which drove them further and further south:

> *Adverse winds repeatedly drove them back; the ship was buffeted again and again by tremendous storms, which seriously damaged her rigging and left the sails in shreds. In mid-ocean she was found to have sprung a leak, and by the beginning of December, after more than two months at sea, she was oozing at every joint and scarcely more than 'half a wreck'. Under such conditions they made no more than 120 miles in three weeks.*

The captain of the ship decided that the continued bad weather was due to Coke's praying and preaching on board. At the height of one storm he paraded the decks, muttering, 'We have a Jonah on board! We have a Jonah on board!' Having worked himself up into a rage, he burst into Coke's cabin, grabbed his books and sermon notes and threw them into the sea. Then, gripping the Doctor, he swore to him that if he prayed or preached again he would be the next thing overboard. Convinced that it would be impossible to reach Halifax in Newfoundland, the captain decided to run before the wind in the hope of making one of the islands of the West Indies. In this way they eventually landed on Antigua on Christmas Day, 1786.

Staggering up the beach towards the town of St John's, Coke bumped into John Baxter, dressed in his clerical gown, on the way to lead a Christmas Day service. Once he had overcome his very natural amazement, Baxter asked Coke to preach.

> *After a little refreshment I went into our chapel, and read prayers, preached, and administered the sacrament. I had one of the cleanest audiences I ever saw. All the negro women were dressed in white linen gowns, petticoats, handkerchiefs and caps. The men were also dressed as neatly. In the afternoon and evening I had very large congregations.*

In America, Coke had ministered to African slaves who formed a third of the country's population. Here, in the West Indies, there were three million black slaves in a population of four million. In Antigua, the influence of the gospel upon the converts was such that for some years it had been no longer necessary to enforce military law over them during the holiday period allowed them over Christmas. They had also become better servants following their conversion. Methodism therefore was highly regarded on the islands. Coke and his companions were very hospitably treated, and he was told that if five hundred pounds would be sufficient to keep him with them it would be forthcoming.

Coke decided to set up what he called 'an Infant Conference'. He received letters from St Vincent's asking for preachers, other letters were given to him recommending him to the governors of St Eustatius and St Kitts. 'All is of God,' he wrote, 'I have no doubt but it would be an open resistance to the clear providences of the Almighty to remove any one of the missionaries at present from this country.'

While Warrener, who was of course intended for Antigua but had arrived there much sooner than anticipated, remained on the island, Coke, Baxter and the other two preachers departed to inspect the neighbouring islands.

They were welcomed at Dominica, St Vincent's, Nevis and St Kitt's. The situation was so encouraging that Coke wrote that the will of God, in respect to the appointment of missionaries there, was as clear as if it had been written with a sunbeam. Clarke was therefore stationed at St. Vincent's and Hammet at St Kitt's. These three men became the first of many missionaries sent out by the Methodists to the West Indian islands.

At St Eustatius, under Dutch rule, they were not given such freedom as in the British dominions. The Dutch would not agree to the establishing of a British mission on their island and after a fortnight's stay Coke departed for America. From this time onwards, the Methodist Conference made provision for the West Indies. On his next three visits to America, Coke stopped off in the West Indies *en route*. His biographer, John Vickers, notes:

> *For thirty years he was to plan and beg and pray without respite for the mission to the slave population of these sun-drenched islands, though the four visits he paid to the Caribbean occupied less than seven months of his time. The name of Thomas Coke remains an inseparable part of the story of West Indian Methodism.*

It is worth emphasizing that this work in Antigua was established many years before the activity of the Baptist Missionary Society, and that Coke's historic landing on the island, with his three missionaries, took place seven years before William Carey's arrival in India in 1793.

In the summer of 1788, Coke brought with him three more missionaries intended for the Caribbean Islands. They landed at Bridgetown, Barbados, and Benjamin Pearce was left there to develop the work. Coke proceeded to St Vincent's, where John Baxter was waiting to welcome him. Another of the preachers was stationed here, and Baxter agreed to become the supervisor of all Methodist work among the Caribbean islands.

Continuing on his circuit, Coke formed a society at Dominica, encouraged the believers at Antigua and St Kitt's, and then again visited St Eustatius. Here, as on the first visit, the circumstances were very different. He had been banned from preaching then but by now even conducting prayer meetings was prohibited. 'This, I think,' wrote Coke, 'is the first instance known among mankind, of a persecution openly avowed against religion itself … it is open and avowedly against *prayer*, the great key to every blessing.' Yet, so strong was the desire of the poor of the island for religious instruction that about two hundred and fifty people met secretly. In the one night that he remained on the island, Coke baptized a hundred and forty of them.

He moved on to the Virgin Islands; with him was William Hammet, who had agreed to leave St Kitts to begin a work in Jamaica. The two men received such a welcome on the islands of Tortola and Santa Cruz that Hammett remained there and Coke sailed on his own to Jamaica. He preached in Kingston and was so well-received that he noted that he had never visited any place, in Europe or in America, where Methodism had not yet been planted, in which he had received such kindness as in Jamaica.

Coke was to visit the Caribbean twice again: in the autumn of 1790 and the autumn of 1792. Each time he brought other missionaries with him. In 1790 he visited Grenada, 'the last of the islands to be opened up by Coke himself'. The Conference held in Antigua in February 1793 was his last in the Caribbean. In the nine years since his first visit the numbers in the societies scattered across the islands had grown from 2,000 to 6,570. There were now twelve missionaries working in ten of the islands. John Vickers summarizes the situation at the time of Coke's death:

> *By 1814 there were twelve circuits throughout the Caribbean, with a membership totalling 17,000. For this, the credit must go, not to Methodism as a whole, but to Thomas Coke.*

A Second Visit to America

From his earlier than expected visit to the Caribbean, Coke proceeded to America, reaching Charleston on 1 March, 1787. He and Francis Asbury, riding together, set out northwards through the Carolinas and Virginia, on a month's preaching itinerary. Often, after preaching at midday, they would still be in the saddle at midnight on their way to the next preaching station.

Coke Chapel, Kingston, Jamaica
Built in 1840 on the site of the first Methodist chapel where Coke preached, it was
severely damaged by an earthquake in 1907 and a new church erected

During this second visit the strong spirit of independence within the American Methodist Church manifested itself. Although they respected Coke personally, the Americans were not willing that their church should be ruled by a British representative (Coke) of a British leader (Wesley). Wesley himself thoroughly deplored this attitude but Coke, having seen the situation in America for himself, was very willing to compromise. He signed a deed of partial abdication 'accepting definite limitations to the exercise of his episcopal powers, and also acknowledging the ultimate authority of the American Conference in the event of Asbury's death.' This document was the equivalent in America of the *Deed of Declaration* in Britain. It meant, for Coke, that his powers in America were limited to presiding over Conference whenever he was in the country and ordaining only those men who had first been appointed by Conference.

The Channel Islands

On leaving Philadelphia on 27 May, Coke sailed to Ireland to meet Wesley in Dublin and to be present at the 1787 Irish Conference. The two men then travelled together to the British Conference in Manchester and they were fellow-travellers again from 10 August to 6 September of that year on a visit to the Channel Islands.

These islands were the second area, after Scotland, mentioned in Coke's *Address* for the support of missionaries. He had visited them before. In January 1786 he had arrived at St Helier, Jersey, and preached in a meeting-room and in the town church. In the absence of a bilingual preacher for Guernsey, a young Methodist preacher from Jersey, Jean de Quetteville, agreed to move to that island. Coke accompanied him and stayed a fortnight on the island, forming a small society and preparing the ground for a mission.

A little over eighteen months later, he was now accompanying Wesley, who, in his eighties, braved the difficult sea passage to the islands for the first time. The company spent some days at both Guernsey and Jersey, preaching as they went and meeting with very different reactions. They were warmly welcomed in Guernsey but at Jersey a drunken mob heckled them; the ringleader assaulted Coke 'in a most brutal and ignominious manner, almost lifting him from the ground by his ears.'

The mission prospered however, so much so that by 1794 Coke could report, 'The societies were formed with such rapidity, that they are now not only able to support the work themselves, but to send money to England to support the general work.'

America again – The Third Visit

Coke arrived at Charleston on his third visit to the United States, having sailed from the Caribbean, on 24 February 1789. He found the work prospering wherever he journeyed in the south: Cokesbury College was now open; a mission among the Indian tribes was planned; at the North Carolina Conference preachers from Kentucky were present, the first time this state had been represented. He heard also of developments further north, where Methodism had been introduced in New England and New York State.

It was during this 1789 visit that Coke first encountered scenes of emotional enthusiasm, which some years later were to develop into the fanatical behaviour of the 'camp-meetings' among the American Methodists. He wrote in his *Journal*:

> *At Annapolis, after my last prayer, the congregation began to pray and praise aloud in a most astonishing manner. At first I found some reluctance to enter into the business; but soon the tears began to flow, and I think I seldom found a more comforting and strengthening time. This praying and praising aloud is a common thing throughout Virginia and Maryland. What shall we say? Souls are awakened and converted by multitudes; and the work is surely a genuine work, if there be a genuine work of God upon earth. Whether there be wildfire in it, or not, I do most ardently wish that there was such a work at this present time in England.*

This reaction was even more common at Baltimore. After the evening service was concluded, 'the congregation began to pray and praise aloud, and continued to do so, till two o'clock in the morning.' It is clear that Coke, though initially uncertain of such behaviour, was willing to allow it to continue. He wrote:

> *Many of our elders who were the softest, most connected, and most sedate of our preachers, have entered with all their hearts into this work. And gracious and wonderful has been the change, our greatest enemies themselves being the judges, that has been wrought on multitudes, on whom the work began at those wonderful seasons.*

Robert Southey, John Wesley's biographer, commented with the benefit of hindsight:

Plainly as it had been shown among the Methodists themselves that emotions of this kind were like a fire of straw, soon kindled and soon spent, the disposition, whenever it manifested itself, was encouraged rather than checked; so strong is the tendency towards enthusiasm. But if Dr Coke, with the advantages of education, rank in life, and of the lessons which he derived from Mr Wesley, when age and long experience had cooled him, could be so led away by sympathy as to give his sanctions to these proceedings, it might be expected that preachers who had grown up in a state of semi-civilization, and were in the first effervescence of their devotional feelings, would go beyond all bounds in their zeal.

An early American camp-meeting

The subsequent history of Methodist camp-meetings, when large crowds were deliberately gathered together and services were prolonged for many hours, specifically in order to produce emotional reactions, justifies Southey's criticism. Even the sagacious Asbury failed to see their dangers. 'We must attend our camp-meetings,' he wrote in 1800, 'they make our harvest time … I hear and see the great effects produced by them.'

On 30 April 1789 George Washington was inaugurated as the first President of the United States. Asbury and Coke, as authorized by the New York Conference of that year, drew up an address congratulating Washington on his appointment, and professing the loyalty of the members of their church. Coke's signature appeared above Asbury's, as 'senior bishop', but it was Asbury who read it out when the two men were granted an audience with the President. It would have been inappropriate for Coke (a British citizen) to have done so. Coke's position throughout the years of his visits to America was difficult. As John Vickers comments,

> The War of Independence was still uncomfortably recent history, and relations between the two countries were still such as to lead to inevitable conflicts of loyalty. Coke was in as difficult a situation as the child of a newly-divorced couple.

Chapter 6: Coke without Wesley

Until 1791 Coke's life, although made up of constant travelling and preaching, had a certain pattern to it. It was based around his three responsibilities – Ireland, America including the West Indies, and administrative and representative work for Wesley in Britain. His routine was to visit Ireland every year and America every two years as he had done in 1785, 1787, 1789 and 1791. His own loyalties and priorities were divided. He generally felt that his main work was to be done in whichever country, America or Britain, he found himself at the time but Wesley's command would always decide for him where he should be. Thus, for example, we find Wesley referring to him in a letter written in 1786: 'I can exceedingly ill spare him from England, as I have no clergyman capable of supplying his lack of service; but I was convinced he was more wanted in America than in Europe.' Wesley's death in 1791 broke up this regular pattern, and though Coke was to visit America on five more occasions, the visits tended to be irregularly spaced and shorter in duration.

The Death of John Wesley

Coke was on his fourth visit to the States when he heard of the death of John Wesley on 2 March 1791. He immediately cut short his visit and proceeded home. It is clear from remarks in some of his letters that he hoped to be appointed President of the Methodist Conference. He had very good reasons for such hopes. According to Vickers, 'The degree of confidence Wesley had placed in him and the number of important commissions entrusted to him inevitably disposed him to expect that he would continue to occupy a key position.' In the time he took to return to Britain, however, many of the senior preachers had met and had agreed on a plan that would avoid the appointment of any successor to Wesley:

There appears to us but two ways, either to appoint another King in Israel; or to be governed by the Conference Plan by forming ourselves into committees. If you adopt the first, who is the Man? What power is he to be invested with? And what revenue is he to be allowed? – But this is incompatible with the Conference Deed.

Their suggestion was accepted in the Conference held that summer. It involved the annual election of a President and other officers, with District Committees administering the decisions of Conference. William Thompson, one of the promoters of the scheme, was appointed the first President.

Secretary of the Methodist Conference

There is perhaps a suggestion of a degree of personal animosity directed at Coke to be seen in the speedy actions of some of the senior preachers at this time. By the alternating arrangement that had been agreed between Wesley and Coke, the 1791 Irish Conference should have been presided over by the former. No provision having been made after his death, the delegates who assembled in Dublin formed themselves into committees and elected one of their own number as chairman: 'In order to give Dr Coke a plain intimation, once for all, that however highly they esteemed and loved him, they could not accept any minister as occupying the exalted position long sustained by the venerable Wesley.' On the other hand, no more might have been involved than what would today be termed 'gesture politics', in that Coke was appointed to preside over the Irish Conference for the following year and almost without exception for every year for the rest of his life. As far as the mainland Conference was concerned, he was elected President for 1797 and 1805. Though determined that no clergyman should any longer be accepted as an autonomous leader of their Society, the Methodists were in no way disposed to lose the energies, abilities and zeal of Thomas Coke. He was immediately appointed Secretary of Conference in 1791 and held that post for many years. Coke was himself very aware of the delicate and crucial nature of the discussions and decisions of this, the first Conference after the death of their leader. His own account of the spirit in which he participated in the proceedings is given in a letter:

> *Our Conference ended in great peace and unanimity. There were innumerable heart-burnings at first: and I saw no way of preserving the unity of the body, but by sacrificing all my little honours which I held in Europe. I accordingly resigned the power which Mr Wesley invested in me … in the management of [his] books, copyrights, etc., and resigned my right to nominate preachers for the new chapel in London … Satan said, 'Divide', but the Spirit of God said, 'Unite'. They gave me leave to visit all the societies in England, appointed me to hold the Conference in Ireland; and authorized me to raise whatever money I might judge necessary for the carrying on of the work in the West Indies, appointing me their Delegate for the West India Islands.*

Coke transferred the duties of various trusteeships to which he had been appointed under the terms of Wesley's will to Conference, so that he might not be seen to be taking matters into his own hands. What meant much more to him were the various commissions he had received from Conference: to be the Conference's 'Delegate' for the West Indies meant, in practice, that he was left in sole charge of Methodist missionaries; to hold the right to raise whatever monies were necessary to carry on the work in the West Indies meant that he was responsible for raising all the funds for Methodist missionary work. At every Conference, for the rest of his life, Coke would make impassioned pleas that he should be given preachers to be stationed at the growing number of mission stations. In most cases, all that he asked for were the men; he himself would provide the finance.

At the request of Conference, he undertook a sixteen-month tour of the United Kingdom preaching on behalf of the West Indian slaves. He asked for contributions when preaching, he applied personally by letters to individuals, he even collected from door-to-door. One navy captain, calling on a friend of Coke's one morning, asked him, 'Do you know anything of a little fellow who calls himself Dr Coke, and who is going about begging money for missionaries to be sent among the slaves? He seems to be a heavenly-minded little devil. He coaxed me out of two guineas this morning.'

He was appointed 'Superintendent of Missions' by Conference, a title that acknowledged the work that he had been doing for some years and, in 1798, a Missions Committee was established to help him in the work. A subsidiary purpose for this committee was for it to act as a moderating influence on Coke's spending. His own choice, in his zeal for overseas mission, would have been to send two or three times as many preachers abroad, but the Committee, mindful of the cost and of competing needs at home, would vote down his more extravagant plans and curb his enthusiasm. Often, when lack of funds required that the Committee refused a particular request, Coke would resort to his own dwindling resources, using the income from properties or selling some government bonds, to make up the need.

Twenty-five years after his death the then President of Conference, Thomas Jackson, wrote of this work:

> Dr Coke ... travelled through the kingdom, making collections in the congregations for their support; soliciting subscriptions from wealthy individuals, wherever he could get access; selecting suitable men for the work, both from the itinerant and the local preachers ... His untiring zeal and perseverance ... eminently qualified him for this difficult and weighty service. For many an imprisoned Missionary in the West Indies did he obtain liberty, by his personal application to men in power; and several persecuting acts of the local legislatures did he prevail upon the Government at home to disallow.

Separation from the Church of England

Inevitably after Wesley's death the question of the relationship between the Methodists and the Church of England arose. As Secretary of the Conference, Coke was intimately involved in all the discussion, arguments and decisions on the matter during the next few years. Many wished Coke to act as a bishop in England, ordaining ministers for the denomination as he had done in America, so that a British Methodist Episcopal Church might result. Conference could not agree to this and forbade all further ordinations until the matter had been decided. Although Coke's sympathies lay with this plan, he obeyed the decision of Conference except in the case of missionaries intended for other countries. He still ordained preachers to be sent to the Caribbean or to France.

At times during these years the different views led to local and national situations of such tension that open controversy within the movement seemed inevitable. Eventually, in 1795, unity was achieved by means of a *Plan of Pacification*, drawn up by Coke, distributed by him to others for their comments, further modified by a committee of all those most involved in the debates, and eventually accepted by the Conference. In this way, the Methodists finally separated from the Established Church after what had been a slow process of innumerable small disengagements. The ten years from Coke's ordination at the hands of Wesley in 1786 to the acceptance of his *Plan of Pacification* in 1795 span the whole history of the long process of Methodist separation.

Thomas Coke in middle age

Events in Ireland

During his 1799 visit to Ireland Coke had to deal with the activities of Lorenzo Dow. This man, the first American revivalist to visit Britain, had been licensed to preach by Francis Asbury but, having little respect for authority, was now on an unauthorized visit to the British Isles. He attempted to introduce American frontier-style revivalism among the Irish Methodist societies. Ten years previously, Coke had welcomed the very first occasions of camp-meetings with a degree of sympathy on his third visit to America, but Dow's more extreme populist and emotionally-charged preaching was a step too far. He was also bringing division into the Irish societies in that the respectable gentry of Dublin wanted nothing to do with the 'Quakerised evangelist', whereas many of those in the countryside admired his style and his success. After failing to convince Dow that his real calling was to missionary work in northern Canada, Coke raised sufficient subscriptions to pay his passage back to America. Dow's return to Britain in 1805 and his subsequent career associated with Hugh Bourne and the birth of the Primitive Methodists is well known, but Coke was not involved with him at this later time.

The various Irish rebellions of the period – that in 1798 in particular – convinced the Methodists that if Ireland was to have peace, then it must be converted to Protestantism. Following a tour through Londonderry, Tyrone and Fermanagh, Coke believed that if this was to be done it would only be through Irish-speaking preachers. He called on the 1799 Irish Conference to send out full-time Gaelic-speaking missionaries, whose main task would be to travel throughout the country preaching to Roman Catholics. Lack of funds was a serious obstacle but Coke pledged himself to raise the funds and two preachers were commissioned.

Coke was completely persuaded of the need for preaching in the vernacular. In a report written in 1801, he stated:

> *Nothing can be more vain or more hopeless than to endeavour to convert a nation by abolishing their language. This method is absurd in the very nature of the thing; for men cannot be instructed, and consequently cannot be converted, by the use of any language but that which they understand: and therefore, if we would convert them, under the Grace of God, we must apply to them in their own language. Every other way is impracticable.*

The work developed rapidly; in ten years there were twelve missionaries operating in six areas, and by 1816 there were twenty-one missionaries, twelve of whom preached in Irish, working on fourteen stations dotted throughout Ireland. In a memorial service held in 1814, after Coke's death, the deep affection in which he was held by Irish Methodists was emphasized.

A Mission to Wales (1800)

Apart from a few individuals, the handful of Wesleyan Methodist societies in North Wales before 1800 were English-speaking groups associated with the Chester Circuit. As he travelled through North Wales, on his frequent journeys to Ireland, Coke became convinced of the spiritual barrenness of this part of his own country. It is true that Calvinistic Methodism, so firmly established in South Wales, had already by 1800 made considerable inroads in the north, but Coke may not have been aware of this or, even if he was, his dislike of Calvinism was so strong that he would not have judged that this was answering the need. His success in Ireland must also have encouraged Coke to make a similar attempt in Wales.

In a later report on Methodist Missions produced at the request of Conference in 1804, Coke wrote, in the third person:

> In travelling annually, for many years, thro' North-Wales … Dr Coke felt exceedingly for his countrymen the Welch, and wished that the everlasting Gospel of Jesus Christ might be preached universally among them. It is true, there are many pious Clergymen in the Churches of Wales, and many Dissenting Ministers in that Principality. But he was, notwithstanding, fully satisfied, that myriads of the Welch were still in spiritual darkness, and lived in the practice of vice, to whom Ministers, on the Itinerant Plan, might find access thro' the blessing of God, when the settled Ministers were not able to reach them … He was at the same time convinced, that no extensive good could be accomplished, unless Itinerant Preachers were found, who were Masters of the Welch Language.

Coke was late in arriving from Ireland at the 1800 London Conference. The circuits for the various preachers for that year had already been confirmed, but for one who, on his own authority, could leave in the West Indies two men who had been appointed by Conference to Newfoundland, the altering of a few schedules was a trivial matter. He had come to London with the set purpose of creating a Welsh Mission. He introduced the subject to the Conference:

> *He related how his heart was being consumed for his kinsmen, the Welsh of North Wales. Did not darkness encompass the land, and were not many being doomed through ignorance? For those preachers already in the country were not interpreting the Gospel broadly enough. Let them hearken unto him therefore, and see if they had not in their midst one who would go among the people of Gwynedd. If such a person would but preach to them in their native tongue, doubtless they would listen to him and return from their erroneous ways.*

In these later years of his life, the Conference's trust and respect for Thomas Coke in all aspects of missionary work was almost complete. They listened with favour to his speech and 'most readily gave him their utmost support'. They set aside two ministers, Owen Davies and John Hughes, for the task, stationing them at Ruthin.

Owen Davies, the Wrexham-born leader of the mission, was given the kind of powers that preachers in other circuits might have envied: 'Brother Davies has a discretionary power to labour as and where he judges best for the advantage of the Mission, and shall have the Superintendence of the whole Mission, and the authority to change the Preachers as he judges best.' He was a cheerful, sensible and paternal man, a good and experienced administrator, but unfortunately was unable to preach in Welsh, though he understood it well enough. John Hughes, like Coke a native of Brecon, was a scholar and antiquarian, but he was a stumbling and indistinct preacher and not much better in Welsh than Davies. That these two men were so unsuitable for the task appointed emphasizes the fact that there were hardly any Welsh-speakers in the ranks of Wesleyan preachers at this time. Yet between them they established societies during that first year in a number of towns and villages around Ruthin with a couple of hundred members in total. John Bryan from Llanfyllin, Montgomeryshire and known as *Bryan bach* ('little Bryan') because of his short stature, joined them after the August 1801 Conference. He was a gifted speaker in his native Welsh, able to move congregations with his powerful preaching.

It is in the context of this Welsh mission that Coke's Arminian understanding of the gospel gave rise to the greatest controversy associated with his ministry. It resulted in the existence of two separate Methodist denominations in Wales.

Y PARCH. OWEN DAVIES.

Y PARCH. JOHN HUGHES.

Calvinistic Methodism and Wesleyan Methodism in Wales

Calvinists, following the teaching of John Calvin (1509-1564) and, before him, of Martin Luther (1483-1546) and Augustine (354-430), believe that the Bible teaches that salvation begins with God's election of his people before the creation of the world. For these, his Church, he sent Christ into the world to suffer as a man and die in their place, receiving in his body and soul the punishment due to them as transgressors of God's holy law. The Holy Spirit provides the gift of faith to the elect so that they come to believe in Jesus Christ. This was the prevalent view in the Western Church from the Protestant Reformation onwards. It was a belief that was contested by the followers of Jacob Arminius (1560-1609), who argued that all men have the ability to choose whether or not to believe Christ's gospel. God foresaw those who would make this choice by faith and on that basis he elected them to be the members of his Church.

The followers of George Whitefield in England, of Jonathan Edwards in America and, in particular, of the Methodists of Wales, led by Daniel Rowland and Howell Harris, were solidly Calvinistic. Wesley's strong and consistent preaching of Arminianism established the theological position of the Wesleyan Methodists. All those who helped and guided Coke in the period in which he came to faith, men like James Browne and John Fletcher, were firmly Arminian, and his great respect for, and loyalty towards, John Wesley confirmed him in this belief. After his appointment as Wesley's assistant, he was hardly ever in Wales, apart from his journeys *in transit* to Ireland, and for this reason together with the fact that he had hardly any understanding of Welsh, it is probable that he never heard the Calvinistic preaching of clergymen such as Daniel Rowland, Peter Williams, David Jones of Llan-gan, David Griffiths of Nevern and others, who were turning Wales upside down. It is unlikely that he ever heard the hymns of William Williams, Pantycelyn, or read the works of Thomas Charles and Thomas Jones, hymns and works that were to

JOHN BRYAN.

establish the majority of Welsh Christians of the first half of the nineteenth century in Calvinistic belief.[1]

The first Wesleyan missioners were received if not with warmth, at least with tolerance. In some places, they were invited to preach in the pulpits of their Calvinistic brethren. Owen Davies, for example, preached very acceptably to the Machynlleth Calvinistic Methodist society. In 1802, Edward Jones of Bathafarn, Denbighshire, joined the mission, enabling it to extend its activity to the west. By March 1803 the society members numbered 1,344. 'There was an element of novelty about their activities as on the occasion in June 1802 in Caernarfon when they had hired the town crier to announce their presence. Not having heard of Wesleyans, he went around the town proclaiming that the Welsh Lions would be preaching that evening.'

It was not long however before the climate changed. More extreme presentations of Arminianism were published, misrepresenting the doctrines of grace. Calvinists responded with equally extreme language and soon a Calvinistic/Arminian pamphlet war was raging in North Wales which was to continue intermittently for some thirty years. This caused a degree of tension between the two Methodist denominations in Wales that was to last for over a hundred years. A good deal of the blame for this must lie at Coke's door for his haste and lack of thought and sensitivity when establishing the mission. In this, he differed from Wesley who had been content to leave Welsh-speaking Wales to the Calvinistic societies of Howell Harris and Daniel Rowland.

The satisfactory growth in the number of Welsh Wesleyans prompted Conference to make administrative changes. Instead of one Ruthin mission attached to the Chester District, two new circuits of Ruthin and Caernarfon were created. By 1810 the Welsh-language circuits had 49 ministers, 60 chapels and 5,549 members.

Darker days were ahead. When Thomas Coke died in 1814 the Welsh Mission lost its most powerful advocate and, over the next decade, there

---

1   The vast majority of the members of the old Dissenters or Nonconformists (the Independents and Baptists) were also of Calvinistic belief.

was a steady seepage of ministers from the Welsh work as support from the Missions Fund dried up. Worse still, Owen Davies, John Bryan, Edward Jones and others were withdrawn and transferred to English circuits. Many societies were left with little pastoral oversight and membership declined year by year so that by 1817 it had fallen to 4,062. Not until the growth associated with the success of Sunday Schools from the mid 1820s onwards was there a gradual recovery of confidence and membership.

In 1935, A. H. Williams, the foremost historian of Welsh Wesleyan Methodism, wrote: 'Wesleyan Methodists in general, and Welsh Wesleyan Methodism in particular, are only now beginning to realize the great work which [Thomas Coke] performed. He bridged the gulf between the death of John Wesley and the rise to power of Jabez Bunting, and is indisputably one of the great figures of Wesleyan Methodist history.'

Last Visits to America

Coke was to visit America five more times after the death of Wesley. The first of these in 1792 was of only a few weeks duration as he hurried on to deal with commitments in the Caribbean. The 1796 visit however revealed the strength of his love for the American Church and his willingness to settle among them if it proved possible to put aside the other calls upon him. With Coke's frequent absences in Europe, the strain of leadership was beginning to tell on Asbury. Seeing this, Coke offered to commit himself wholly to America; he asked only for permission to 'visit the West Indies, and France when there is an opening, when I can be spared.' This offer was accepted and when he sailed home to Britain he carried with him a letter asking the British Conference that he might be released from his responsibilities. While he waited for the 1797 Conference, Coke began to wind down his personal affairs and arrange his finances. The considerable wealth inherited from his father had, by now, nearly all gone. The various properties had been sold as one financial need after another had arisen in the various missions for which he was responsible. On 5 April, he wrote to a friend:

Now I am going to take my leave of Europe, I will inform you of my temporal circumstances: by the considerable sums which I have myself given from time to time in my zeal for the preaching of the Gospel in the differing parts of the world, I shall not have any more of my fortune remaining, after settling all my affairs, than the Coity Mortgage, if you except my library, which may be worth two or three hundred pounds.

However the British response to the letter from America was to appoint him to the Presidency of the Conference for the forthcoming year, and in their reply to their overseas brethren they stressed that the difficult circumstances in Britain since the death of Wesley meant that it was still too early to dispense with Coke's aid.

Another very brief visit, in November 1797, involved little more than delivering this message to the American Conference. Again in 1800, his American visit accounted for little more than explaining for a second time that the Methodist leaders in Britain judged that they could not do without him at that time. The responding letter from America this time noted: 'We have, therefore, in compliance with your request, *lent* the Doctor to you for a season, to return to us as soon he conveniently can, but at farthest, by the meeting of our next General Conference.' As John Vickers notes, 'The exchange of official courtesies had reached a point at which neither side was quite certain who was lending to whom.' Seeing the way the wind was blowing, however, the Americans at this time appointed a third bishop over their church, Richard Whatcoat, the first preacher ordained by Wesley for America, as an assistant to the aging Asbury.

During Coke's visits to America, the finances of the missions always suffered. Although the other members of the Mission Committee were meant to take over the fund-raising in his absence, this never took place. At this period also, Coke was giving more and more of his time to writing a commentary on the Bible. Because the missions were his over-riding priority throughout these years, he was beginning to realize that it was never going to be possible for him to give himself entirely to America. Before he set sail on his ninth and last visit, the British Conference again sent the message that because 'of the state of our several Missions, and various other forcible reasons that might be mentioned,' it was necessary that he should return.

Coke arrived in Virginia at the end of October 1800. During this visit he preached his way from Charleston as far as Boston. He visited Rhode Island for the first time. He was invited to preach before the American Congress in Washington, and he spoke on 'the wisdom, dignity, and importance of the gospel, as contrasted with the spirit of the world.' By the time he left for home, it had become clear that Asbury was no longer willing to share the leadership with a fellow bishop who was only present in America for a tenth of his time, and that Coke himself was not willing to abandon all his work in Europe in exchange for becoming no more than an additional itinerating preacher in the American backwoods. Although neither realized that this would be the last visit and that they would not see each other again, they knew that their old partnership, as Wesley's two bishops over American Methodism, had come to an end. When Coke died, Asbury spoke of him as the greatest of all British Methodists, greater even than Wesley himself. From an American point of view, this was an accurate assessment.

Chapter 7: Marriage, Literary Work and Asia

Further Missions: France, Sierra Leone and Gibraltar

One motivation for the missions Coke had established in the Channel Islands was the strong hope that they might provide the stepping stone for an 'invasion' of the mainland. The continuing consequences of the French Revolution in 1789 put paid to any immediate fulfilment of that hope. However, in 1791, he ordained Jean de Quetteville in Jersey and took him to start a mission in France. They rode to Paris and Coke announced a service, to be held in a meeting-house on the banks of the Seine. Only six turned up to hear him and very soon he was dealing with death threats. Disappointed, he and his friends retreated to Normandy, where de Quetteville established a work which was to develop into the basis of Methodist activities in France. In 1794, Coke was still hopeful of contributing to the French work and made great efforts to improve his French.

In 1796, Coke sent out four married and two single preachers to begin a work in Sierra Leone. In this instance, however, he had not chosen his missionaries wisely, nor prepared them adequately for African life. Changing their minds on seeing the conditions under which they were to work, the party of ten all returned to Britain. Coke remained convinced of the importance of establishing a work in Africa. He had been struck by the promise: 'Ethiopia shall soon stretch out her hands unto God' (Psalm 68:31), and preached often on this text during his itineraries. Eventually, under the leadership of George Warren in 1811, a mission was established which laid the foundations of a permanent Methodist work in West Africa.

In 1804, Coke sent out a preacher and his wife to help a society of fifty in Gibraltar. These both died of the yellow fever within a year, but another man, William Griffiths, was sent there in 1807 to continue their work.

Marriage

The main reason Coke never returned for a tenth visit to America was that he got married. In November 1804 he wrote to the Missions Committee that 'a lady, whose name, I think, I am not at liberty to mention just at present at least … has promised me *one hundred guineas* for the missions.' By January, this same lady had donated a further hundred guineas. Her name was Penelope Smith, the daughter of a successful solicitor of Bradford, Wiltshire, from whom she had inherited a considerable fortune: 'a deeply pious, simple-hearted woman.' They married in April 1805. He was 57 years old and she was in her mid-40s. They were very deeply attached to one another. Rather than being apart from her husband, Penelope accompanied him on all his longer tours. In the first six weeks of marriage they journeyed four hundred miles together. Three years later, Coke wrote to Asbury, 'We are always travelling, and I annually visit and preach at more places than I did for many years before my marriage.'

Penelope brought her love and her money to the marriage. Coke's own wealth had been decimated, as noted, and the Missions Committee had no funds remaining. His wife, however, was as open-handed as he was. Her house was sold and the two of them lived on the road, depending on the hospitality of others. Her money saved the Committee from a bankruptcy which would have resulted in draconian cutbacks in many of the Methodist missions. However, in 1809, a stormy crossing of the Irish Sea brought on a prolonged fever from which Penelope never fully recovered and she died in January 1811. She is buried in Brecon Cathedral. Coke, in his grief, threw himself into renewed fund-raising preaching tours.

Before the end of 1811, Coke married again. Both he and Penelope had been friends of Anne Loxdale, a prominent member of the society at Liverpool. Some of her family objected to the marriage because her health was so poor. Unfortunately, their fears were realized; Anne died a few days short of their first wedding anniversary.

Literary Work

From the moment he was engaged as Wesley's assistant, Coke was obliged to be continually writing: travelling journals, administrative and legal letters, innumerable pamphlets and some sermons flowed from his pen. Once his responsibility for the missions began, the countless missionary reports were added to this output. It might be thought that in such a constantly busy life there would be no time to produce any substantial work. But Coke did have periods of complete inactivity in which he could write, particularly his long Atlantic crossings to America, and he used these to the full.

He produced two major works. His *History of the West Indies* was produced in three volumes (1808, 1810 and 1812). This comprised 'the natural, civil and ecclesiastical history of each island: with an account of the missions instituted in those islands, from the commencement of their civilization.' The work to which he gave his greatest time and attention was his *Commentary on the Bible*. This was begun at the request of the 1792 Conference for a commentary that would not be as long as those of Matthew Henry and John Gill, but longer than Wesley's *Commentary*. Although initially planned as a three-volume work it grew to six volumes, the first appearing in 1801 and the sixth in 1807. It was the profits that he made from the sale of this work that enabled him to continue paying his own expenses and to contribute to missionary needs in those years between the draining of his own fortune and his marriage to Penelope. Spurgeon's view of the commentary was not at all complimentary:

> *A Wesleyan comment. Too big: ought to have been put in half the space. Moreover, it is next door to a fraud, for it is 'in the main a reprint of the work of Dr Dodd', without that author's name. Ah, Dr Coke, this is a burning shame!*

This is an unfortunate allegation. Coke had made no claim to originality; the work is a compilation drawn from many sources. In his *Advertisement to the Reader*, intended for the commentary, Coke noted that his sources included: 'Mr Henry, Dr Dodd, Dr Haweis, Bishop Hopkins, Mr McEwen, etc., etc.,' For some reason the publishers did not include this advertisement. This was the commentary most used by Wesleyan Methodists until Adam Clarke's *Commentary* was completed in 1825. An abridged version was translated into Welsh (Old Testament, 1808; New Testament, 1813).

Asia and the Last Voyage

The vision of a Methodist mission to the East had impressed itself upon Coke as early as 1784. He had discussed the matter with Wesley but the pressing needs of America overtook both of them and the plan was shelved. Throughout the years, however, Coke nurtured the thought, keeping up with all the information about religious developments in India and corresponding with directors of the East India Company. In 1805 he began lobbying his friends in government – William Wilberforce, Lord Teignmouth, Lord Castlereagh – appealing for their support. The directors of the East India Company, however, concerned only with their commercial interests, refused to allow a mission. Coke knew them well enough to state: 'We must wait an age, if we wait for the vote of the Indian Court of Directors. Those merchants are princes and quite above the gospel.'

But Ceylon was a different case. Unlike India, it was under direct British rule and Coke's friends in government could use their influence to raise awareness of the need for such a mission. In April 1813, he persuaded the Missions Committee to recommend to Conference that missionaries be sent to the Cape of Good Hope and to Ceylon. Coke himself was designated the General Superintendent of the Asiatic Mission. But he wished for more than this: he wanted to go to Asia himself, though he was now sixty-six years old:

> I am now dead to Europe, and alive for India. God himself has said to me, 'Go to Ceylon'. I am as much convinced, that methinks I had rather be set naked on the coast of Ceylon, without clothes, and without a friend, than not go there.

In the July 1813 Conference, he made a passionate speech, asking for twelve men to be sent out. The cost involved was too much for Conference to agree. He therefore offered £6,000 from his own pocket, and this seems to have shamed his brethren to respond. They agreed to finance seven men for Ceylon, one for Java and one for the Cape of Good Hope, with Coke paying only for the equipment of the party. Coke began learning Portuguese, there being no Singhalese or Tamil tutors to be found in London. His plan was to establish Ceylon as the headquarters for the work in Asia, and then to visit Madras, Calcutta and, perhaps, Java, before returning home, after some two and a half years, to report. His one great anxiety was the knowledge that fund-raising for the missions would decline again in his absence. He was greatly encouraged by the work of a thirty-three year old man from Manchester, Jabez Bunting, who had helped form a District Missionary Society in Leeds with the aim of obtaining regular subscriptions. Bunting was to be the main administrator of missionary work after Coke's death and from 1830 until his own death in 1858, the foremost statesman of Wesleyan Methodism.

The party sailed from Portsmouth on 30 December 1813. His work for the weeks of voyaging ahead of him was the preparation of a new edition of a Portuguese Bible which he intended to publish on arrival at Ceylon. The violence of the storms delayed them while in Madeira and it was the end of April before they rounded the Cape and sailed up the east coast of Africa as far as Madagascar. As they again approached the heat of the tropics, Coke became unwell. On the morning of 3 May, his servant found him dead on his cabin floor. The ship's doctor certified his death as due to an apoplectic fit, brought on by working too hard at his studies under tropical conditions. 'His fellow-missionaries noted the placid smile which still rested on his features when they entered his study.'

He was buried at sea, that same day, at latitude 2 degrees 29 south, and longitude 59 degrees 29 east, that is, about 430 miles north-east of the northernmost point of Madagascar. The ship sailed on, delivering the missionaries to Ceylon. Within five years the Portuguese New Testament was printed and the whole of the Bible translated into Singhalese. By 1817, missions were successfully established in Mysore and Bangalore, and, ten years later, in Calcutta.

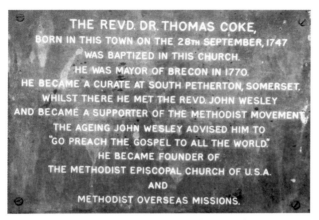

Memorial plaque outside St Mary's Church, Brecon

Chapter 8: Final Thoughts

Coke's Missionary Methods

It is interesting to compare Coke's missionary methods, which were at the very beginning of modern missionary activity, with those of today, two hundred years later. There are obvious differences of course, but also much that is surprisingly similar.

Coke was very careful in choosing those whom he would send out. It was not enough that a man should volunteer for the work. Those selected by Coke had already passed through one vetting procedure in that they had been accepted as preachers of the Methodist Conference. Furthermore, Coke worked hard to ensure that it was the best of these that he secured as his missionaries. Wesley would sometimes complain of him that he asked for the most promising men from the lists of both circuit and local preachers.

The attitude of cultural arrogance and snobbery, so often associated with colonization, was present of course, to some extent, in many of the early missionaries. It is hard to say to what degree Thomas Coke was affected by such prejudices. It is clear, however, that they did not blind him to the many faults of the colonial system. Very soon after arriving in America he sympathized with their fight for independence as a country. He was quickly persuaded that Wesley's directions for the development of the Methodist societies in America were foreign to the situation, and within weeks of landing on American shores he had helped to establish an independent American Episcopal Methodist Church.

In his vehement opposition to black slavery he fought against the majority view of fellow-Methodists in America and fellow-Britons in the West Indies. He would not accept that there was any merit in their economic or cultural arguments. The missions he established in the various islands of the West Indies were nearly all societies made up of black congregations and from the beginning he made use of black preachers. The vision of Ethiopians stretching out their hands to God was very real to him: when travelling to raise funds in Britain he constantly emphasized the duty of the British people, in the light of their oppression of the slaves, to contribute money in order that the gospel of salvation in Jesus Christ might be sent to them.

While Coke was perhaps less affected by colonial prejudices than many, he was not so free of that other prejudice, which has been termed 'tribalism': bringing one's own denominational culture and beliefs into a missionary context where other views already prevail. His dislike of Calvinism prejudiced him against the various Reformed denominations of his day but this was not relevant with respect to most of his missionary work. While he travelled through virgin territories in the southern states of America, or from island to island in the West Indies his preaching was often the first proclamations of the gospel to those parts and he was free to set up that form of church order which accorded with his own understanding of Scripture. He should, however, have appreciated that the establishing of a periodical, 'The Arminian Magazine', in the eastern and northern states of America, where Puritan influence was still strong, or the aggressive approach of his missions in the midst of his Calvinistic Methodist brethren in Wales, was bound to cause friction.

Coke's gifts enabled him, almost on his own, to set up a successful scheme of missionary activity, operating in many countries. For years he acted as Home Director, Field Director, Financial Director, Fund Raiser and Literature Officer. This, of course, could not continue indefinitely. After some years the Missions Committee had to be appointed with the immediate task of regulating the financial structure. As the numbers of missionaries grew, the Committee assumed more and more responsibility. In 1818, four years after his death, the formation of the *General Wesleyan Methodist Missionary Society* ensured that the missions continued to operate as an organic part of the Methodist Church.

Coke's Character

On hearing of Coke's death, Francis Asbury wrote: 'Jealousy, malice, or envy, dwelt not in a soul as noble as that of Coke … A gentleman, a scholar, and a bishop to us; and as a minister of Christ, in zeal, in labours, in services, the greatest man in the last century.' Asbury was aged twenty-six when he left England for America and would have known the Wesley brothers. In all his years in America he would have learnt much of the ministries of George Whitefield, Jonathan Edwards, David Brainerd and others. But to Francis Asbury, Coke was 'the greatest man of the eighteenth century'. We do not have to agree with him in this judgment, but his comment is evidence of the fact so often mentioned in biographies of Coke, that he was greatly loved in many countries. His congregations in other lands knew, so much more than his many hearers in Britain, the circumstances he had to endure to bring the gospel of peace to them: the thousands of miles on horseback through the forests, swamps and rivers of America, the heat and humidity of the West Indies, the danger from mobs in these two countries and in the Channel Islands, and from rebellions in Ireland and, over and above these, the very real danger of loss of life involved in every one of his eighteen crossings of the Atlantic in the small wooden ships of his day. His own love for his overseas hearers – colonialists, frontiersmen, peasants and slaves – is evident from the great difficulty he had in parting from them as his responsibilities in England pulled him away so many times.

On the other hand, we have to consider the accusations of ambition, self-seeking and arrogance that followed him and have been repeated often by later historians. There is no doubt that he was impulsive, impatient, apt to take too much upon himself, and sometimes rash in his judgments, both of events and of his fellow-men. His liberality with his own money meant that at times he did not pay enough attention to the demands of financial restraints nor to the requirements of strict book-keeping and this understandably aroused the anger and suspicion of many of his brethren and colleagues. Such criticisms are often found in the writings of those who encountered him in his early years. There are others, however, who wrote of him after his death who provide a more rounded picture. We see this, for example, in the views of a man who followed him as President of the Methodist Conference, Thomas Jackson (1783-1873). He stated, in 1839:

> *Everyone who knew him was aware that his judgment was not equal to his zeal. The ardour of his mind sometimes bordered upon impetuosity, and occasionally led him, especially in the absence of his ordinary advisers, into acts of indiscretion. This was his great failing; and he often confessed it...*
>
> *[But] to the cause of religion and humanity he devoted all that he had to give – his property, his time, his intellect, his influence, his life ... He might have purchased a rich living, and probably have obtained preferment in the Church, had he been so minded. Instead of this, he lived only to promote the spiritual interests of the most neglected of mankind.*

This slightly ambiguous testimony of those who knew him is perhaps best understood by realizing that what we find in Coke's life is a typical example of that growth in grace by the work of the Holy Spirit which, to some degree or other, is seen in the lives of all believers. In his first years, as a wealthy, gifted, privileged and indulged young man, as a curate, as a Methodist convert, even as Wesley's right-hand man, he displayed a self-centredness, self-confidence and ambition which undoubtedly caused offence to many. On more than one occasion he revealed the strength of his desire to be a bishop. One suspects that he enjoyed the authority that Wesley's patronage gave him. But as the years passed, with their accompanying disappointments and crushed hopes, and particularly as he was increasingly convicted of the urgent need of the gospel for those who were in darkness, so we see his priorities changing. His wealth, energies and time were devoted increasingly to the two callings that pressed most upon him: the preaching of the gospel and the planting of Christian societies. As he left Britain on his final voyage, the following were among his last words:

We go forth in the name of God, trusting solely to him for the success which we hope to realize ... For my own part, I am fully persuaded, that we, who are about to leave you, are in the path of duty; and I am perfectly convinced that God will bless our labours ... It is of little consequence whether we take our flight to glory from the land of our nativity, from the trackless ocean, or the shores of Ceylon ... We can appeal to heaven for the purity of our motives, and we look into eternity for our reward.

Plaque outside his birthplace in High Street, Brecon

Commemoration

There are two notable monuments to Thomas Coke. The first is the plaque in Wesley's Chapel, City Road, London, commemorating his life and work. It is appropriate that in this place, where he so often preached to London Methodists or presided over Methodist Conferences, alongside the memorials for John Wesley, Charles Wesley, John Fletcher, Jabez Bunting and other leading Methodist fathers, there should be a worthy reminder of 'The Father of Methodist Missions'. The second monument is a large plaque, full of the details of his life, in the nave of Brecon Cathedral, where so often as a boy he would have worshipped with his family, and where he would have officiated in mayoral responsibilities as a young man, long before he had any thoughts of being a missionary for Jesus Christ all over the globe.

Plaque in Brecon Cathedral

Thomas Coke memorial in Wesley's Chapel, City Road, London

Further Reading

1. Davey, Cyril, *Mad about Mission: The Story of Thomas Coke, Founder of the Methodist Overseas Mission* (London: Marshall Pickering, 1985), 127 pages. A very readable popular biography.

2. Vickers, John, *Thomas Coke: Apostle of Methodism* (London: Epworth Press, 1969; reprint Wipf and Stock: 2013), 394 pages. A very full, readable, meticulously researched biography. The definitive life of Thomas Coke.

3. Williams, A. H., *Welsh Wesleyan Methodism, 1800-1858* (Bangor: Llyfrfa'r Methodistiaid, 1935). Pages 45-132 provide a detailed account of Coke's involvement in the establishing of the Welsh Methodist mission.

Jamaican 1989 commemorative stamp